THE SAME SEA, THE SAME GLOAMING

"MEN WANTED: FOR HAZARDOUS JOURNEY. SMALL WAGES, BITTER COLD, LONG MONTHS OF COMPLETE DARKNESS. CONSTANT DANGER, SAFE RETURN DOUBTFUL. HONOUR AND RECOGNITION IN EVENT OF SUCCESS."

—Sir Ernest Shackleton, recruitment ad for the Imperial Trans Antarctic Expedition aboard the *Endurance*, December 29, 1913

The Same Sea,
   the Same Gloaming

Poems

EUGENE O'CONNOR

Copyright © 2018 Eugene O'Connor.
All rights reserved.
Published by Williams & Co. Books, Columbus, OH.

Cover image: Odilon Redon, *La Tête d'Orphée, ou Le Noyé* (*The Head of Orpheus, or The Drowned Man*), charcoal drawing, 1887. Rijksmuseum, Amsterdam. Used with permission.

Cover design and text design by Juliet Williams.

The Same Sea,
the Same Gloaming

Poems

EUGENE O'CONNOR

Copyright © 2018 Eugene O'Connor.
All rights reserved.
Published by Williams & Co. Books, Columbus, OH.

Cover image: Odilon Redon, *La Tête d'Orphée, ou Le Noyé* (*The Head of Orpheus, or The Drowned Man*), charcoal drawing, 1887. Rijksmuseum, Amsterdam. Used with permission.

Cover design and text design by Juliet Williams.

To Ken, with love

To Allan, in loving memory

CONTENTS

I. DARKNESS, LIGHT

Poking the Possum	3
Green Tea	4
Louise Nevelson's Boxes	5
Low Light Makes for Understanding	6
Lupus in Fabula (The Wolf in the Tale)	7
The Flood Subject: A Parable of Thieves	8
The Same Sea, the Same Gloaming	9
Aubade	10

II. CINDERS, HOSTAGES

Winter Concern	13
The Fox	14
A Spider Wasp Feasts on a Wolf Spider	16
Clouds	17
The Afterlife of the Marcel	18
Hostages	19
In This Dying City	20
The River Runs Cold	21
Ashes	22
Broken Wing	23

III. ICE FLOES, SALT

A Christmas Poem	27
"One wintertime, the snow ..."	28
Shipwreck	29
Making Snow Angels	31
"It snowed overnight ..."	32
Winter: Mo(u)rning	33

Snow	34
"This is a major storm, it has life and death implications."	35
Farther Out	36
Lot's Wife in Reverse	37
Acknowledgments	*39*
About the Author	*41*

I.
Darkness, Light

Poking the Possum

It was a marriage of heaven and hell:
lured from the green shade   its clover scent
and apple blossom it darted out
into the road toward a promise
of fruit overripe in a sack gone moist
owing to our neglect and waste.

Satiety was offered and denied
in a moment of carelessness and haste
before we knew what animal it was—
before we'd tasted the fruit
of paradise—

we longed to dream, and forget.

Green Tea

Its essential properties are:
emerald, jade, deep, reflective pools
the color of your eyes.

Its consumption is legendary:
first brewed during the dynasty
of Emperor Chen Nung. To brew

and serve it requires care
and patience. Too hot, too cool
and it's ruined. Balance is key.

So the jade, the emerald, the color
of your eyes. So too gossamer,
translucent cups. My grandmother's

upturned bowl, held there
by habit or a finer grace,
learning to be content

with little, with the ghosts
of things.

Louise Nevelson's Boxes

There is a power to plain objects.
There is no mystery   no stay
or run. No other way
but further in

past the cold shoals of grief   robbed
of distance and perspective

the blunt, brute surface
of the midnight sky   the moon's
damp spur

I go in.
I go under.

Low Light Makes for Understanding

The moon shines ordinary past
the house and barn. Pale clouds
shift nonchalantly overhead. Little help
is offered by the full lamps, making
the surrounding dark seem
darker still.

It's true, the moon shines clear enough
that I can see it whole, pocked
and cratered, its dark side bulldozed
like a quarry that they've scoured for coal.
And in that I feel a sense of solace,
even gratitude, for its inadequacies.

With such ravages might come experience,
call it wisdom, maybe, resignation: a slow
drift down the road toward a deeper place
where I might settle, and see nothing,
and chide myself because
I had not seen it sooner.

Lupus in Fabula (The Wolf in the Tale)

It steals along
and speaks in reedy voices.
Moon bright, it lurks
in its shadow.

If you were a fig
you would be in my mouth.
If you were a bird,
you would utter prophecies.

Draw lots, separate
the crushed leaves, divine
the tale it leaves in footprints
in the snow.

The Flood Subject: A Parable of Thieves

Early winter mornings I hear them:
the crows gathered in their thousands.
Imagine: bare tree branches thick
with their dark bodies, the tide water
of their constant droppings. Noah's Flood:
the crowding together, the uneasy passage
over water before being moored on Ararat.

In this place of parable the characters speak
as one of their desire for slick, shiny surfaces—
keys, foil, anything that gleams among
the shadows. I picture the fan of wings,
the grasping beak.

Every morning I return to it: the flood subject,
buoyed, then inundated, by thoughts
of profit, of getting out of bed to shave,
to dress, to find the set of keys I thought
I'd lost owing to my carelessness, to the air,
to night, to the blue-black murder
of departing crows. They call to me.
They recognize me as they go.

Lupus in Fabula (The Wolf in the Tale)

It steals along
and speaks in reedy voices.
Moon bright, it lurks
in its shadow.

If you were a fig
you would be in my mouth.
If you were a bird,
you would utter prophecies.

Draw lots, separate
the crushed leaves, divine
the tale it leaves in footprints
in the snow.

The Flood Subject: A Parable of Thieves

Early winter mornings I hear them:
the crows gathered in their thousands.
Imagine: bare tree branches thick
with their dark bodies, the tide water
of their constant droppings. Noah's Flood:
the crowding together, the uneasy passage
over water before being moored on Ararat.

In this place of parable the characters speak
as one of their desire for slick, shiny surfaces—
keys, foil, anything that gleams among
the shadows. I picture the fan of wings,
the grasping beak.

Every morning I return to it: the flood subject,
buoyed, then inundated, by thoughts
of profit, of getting out of bed to shave,
to dress, to find the set of keys I thought
I'd lost owing to my carelessness, to the air,
to night, to the blue-black murder
of departing crows. They call to me.
They recognize me as they go.

The Same Sea, the Same Gloaming

Conversation comes to a stop
and we just wait and listen
for the turning of the light.

I watch for the two of us
and say it with my fingers.
You turn to find a line of fiery red—

This synchronous slow burning:
it breaks the impasse
we had each felt looking out:

the repetitious turning of the lights
and parallel wide streets. The same
sea, the same gloaming.

Aubade

What we knew once: hopefulness,
the air we breathed again
following the flood,
goes the way of fissures
and canyons.

We lie too deep down in the shadow here.

It's spring, time to renew
those same desperate vows:
certainty of what's ahead
even if the way is lost.

Sky grows brighter—
it begets blood—
it gets visual

II.
Cinders, Hostages

Winter Concern

Old trees are witnesses:
   Their simple religion is forced into the cold,
   No intermediary gives them rules of conduct:
   All day without a minister they hold
Primitive services.
—THOM GUNN, "A KIND OF ETHICS"

The trees are branches now, the fields
fallow. Soon the snow. But
not yet. The skies are clear
and unconcerned, storm clouds
still far off. Peaceful all is.

Standing still, the line of trees
as if to know how quickly sky
can change. Traffic on the distant
highway hums, a train of two
freights cargo to its destination.

Everything is staid and as it should:
no fracture, no release or panic,
yet, over the trouble men might do,
their callousness and longing to destroy
for an idea. Because they can.

The Fox

The more strongly I smelled the lion, the more loudly I sang.
—LEONORA CARRINGTON, SURREALIST PAINTER AND
SCULPTOR, FABULIST, INCORRIGIBLE ECCENTRIC (1917–2011)

I thought I heard it scuffling
in the dune grass just outside
the window of the room where I slept.
But there was no sleeping.

I had seen it already, at dusk: its snout,
its long tail tipped with white,
approaching me. They get so tame around people,
rummaging in their bins and bowls.

This leaves out the occasional kill: birds
or small rodents, fresh blood.
The dune grass shook in the ripening wind.
I heard the occasional bird cry.

Stars and moonlight grazed
my face. I caught my reflection
in the glass. Caught: the operative word.
Caught: in a circle of pale light.

Then came the sound of its movement,
the soft pad of its feet on sand.
Do foxes bark or cry out, I wondered.
Is theirs a song of nurture or abandonment?

*There was the parable I sang, of the fox
with red hair who lurks outside a barn
while lambs are sleeping. One day the fox
would end up trapped inside the barn—*

*I carried the story up and down
the Yellow Star House, to buoy the others
up. It lifted their spirits if not their fate:
the last transport carried them instead.*

*The louder they sang the more
they smelled the lion and not the lamb.
The smell of the lion, its yellow eyes
and red mouth open wide—*

A Spider Wasp Feasts on a Wolf Spider

The larva of a spider wasp infests
the body of a wolf spider stunned
by the wasp mother, its rear legs
bitten off so its large abdomen
hugs the ground, though it remains
alive through all this, fresh
for the kill—

The spider's four rear legs
bitten off, the four in front
pluck the air like a violoncello.
Writhing and helpless
as a baby on a changing table.

Funny thing to happen
to a spider when normally
the scenario runs: *Come into
my silk parlor, says the spider
to the unsuspecting fly* . . .

Today's lesson: anybody can be prey
for those who gain
by plundering the disadvantaged
and the dying.

Ask the wasp, dying itself
to test its brand-new pincers,
ready to tuck in . . .

Clouds

—inspired by Alfred Stieglitz's cloud photos, collectively titled "Equivalents," a decade-long project photographed during summers at Lake George, New York

They may be wind-sprung.
They may be blown away
the way some people are
by violence impelled.

I shall never have the skill
to fly. I must therefore
choose myself some other way,
take myself off so not to share

in this anxiety as busy yet
as lonely as men remaining
at the border of the ebbing tide
to go no farther nor to sail away

as clouds do to reveal the sky
and sun as it declines like tragic
cargo every evening past
the islands on the other side.

The Afterlife of the Marcel

The Marcel Wave (sometimes spelled Marcelle) is a stylish wave given to the hair by means of heated curling irons. Named for François Marcel, nineteenth-century French hairdresser who invented the process in 1872. It revolutionized the art of hairdressing all over the world and remained in vogue for over fifty years, making a fortune for Mr. Marcel. Originally known as the "Undulation Marcel," the name evolved to the "Marcel Wave."
—1920-1930.COM

It was youth they saw.
It was an elegance: waves tight
to the scalp and undulating down,
edged with a razor at the back
where the hairline ended.

Ended, their youth, long ago,
as I remember these old women. They held on
to the flapper cut, though their hair
was white now, and their lives
were edged with loss and sorrow.

In that photo of my grandmother
she gazes frontally and smiles,
her blue-white hair crisped
in a Marcel. She looks for all
the world at peace and calm.

No hint of the war, one son across,
another dead. No hint of rage
or sorrow.

Think ridges, think oceans' slow decline
and sigh at the shore's edge
following a gale that's swallowed
boats and sails cascading down
in ripples   ripples
lashed with spume and spray.

Hostages

Grosgrain clouds slip
beneath the horizon
like pillows falling
off a bed.

Luxurious things fall
into dirt and pool
in cisterns. Dry leaves float
on the surface.

The pale hostages
leave the wind-raked field,
the barn and stables visible
just beyond.

They arrive without shoes.
They arrive without
their children. They lean
against each other
like drunken houses.

In the yellow grass
the scarecrow still
extends its arms—

The wind escaping
through the narrow trees
tears madly
at its clothes.

In This Dying City

Nights gather cold,
without shelter. In this dying city
all who remain are childless.

They've lost their children twice,
as in an Orphic tale. The danger
lay in looking back.

They eat no food
but ashes. People huddle
in what clothes they have.

They look on at that woman
in black, tragic as the days
of privation.

The way she walks, the veil
covering her face.

The River Runs Cold

Sky's arc   the river
runs cold as a saint's blood.

Nothing else stirs. It is winter
in its stillness.

There is hunger   everywhere
the unifying force of food is broken.

A thrum of darkness moves along-
side morning light.

It is winter   in its stillness
and there is nothing but stones to eat.

Ashes

In Cienfuegos, land of fires.
At the Church of the Virgin
and its bells, statues of saints
wear white lace dresses
or painted garments of gold.

Gazing up or out, with haloes
like bonnets and fingers extended,
some broken off. They have a right
to be sad at that age.

At a side altar
Christ already with his crown
of thorns and seated
on a throne of ashes

sitting down as if to ask himself
whether it's worth it; whether
death by any other means . . .

How do you measure loss?
how many ashes
does it take the turn the black
clothes white?

Count the number of stars
in the black sky: that many

Broken Wing

—for those killed in a gas attack in Syria, April 4, 2017

A shoulder's frail
wing shows above
the blanket

fragile and cold
as an ice shelf
broken off.

Ammar
Aya
Mohammed
Ahmad. I love you
my birds.

Aunt Sana
Uncle Yasser
Abdul-Kareem.
Please hear me.

A father carries
his twin babies to be
buried with their mother.

My birds, he calls out
to them. Past them.
To the sky.

More come, ever more.
The pickup trucks
are high with bodies.

They were dead.
I saw them.
All are dead now.

The twin babies look asleep,
look like dolls. They shall lie
with their mother.

They will rot
with their mother
in their cold earth bed.

III.
Ice Floes, Salt

A Christmas Poem

Rime thickens the grasses,
ice coats tree branches.
Gray days continue with
their constant narrative.

Old-fashioned Christmases,
the kind we see in movies:
were they ever so idyllic?
Must we eat lotus to forget?

You have cried once too often.
Hoarfrost coats the grasses.
Tell me: if sorrow is moisture
what else is happiness but drought?

"One wintertime, the snow . . ."

One wintertime, the snow
fell constantly. It stayed twilight
until full darkness unrelieved
by moonlight, starlight.

We scanned the paper:
war, a man poleaxed his wife
& kids, his brain riven by the ice
against his window.

Blame it on the fact the lights
went out for weeks & I a boy
would light the candles every day
at dusk.

The culprits were sponge baths
& boredom, huddling around
the stove for warmth & light
too poor to read by.

The house began to smell
of tallow & candle wax.
We learned to be hoarders
of our borrowed light.

Crude cave fire
and the outer dark.
The table set
on dirty oilcloth, we sit.

The eating starts.

Shipwreck

[The ship] is slowly giving up her sentient life. I cannot write about it.
—FROM SIR ERNEST SHACKLETON'S DIARY

1.
Pity Shackleton. Pity Shackleton
and his crew, their ship foundering
& lost and they stranded here. They take
photos of themselves, their cat,
their ship as well, the ship that
brought them, its sails

unfurled but hanging limp & torn,
the mast swaying, listing
with the rest of it. The photos
show them smiling, smiling
through their unkempt beards,
through their gritted teeth, even.

Before their end comes
they look long distances away
toward the edge of the ice
where the sun plants itself,
then darkens and dies.

2.
Oh pity us, Shackleton, we
who are left
on this sinking, sodden ground,
the sea's salt encroaching
and the ground no longer able
to hold us securely, the buildings . . .

Things grow stiff & heavy with salt.
We don't dare look back, as Lot's wife did,
or we will be brought low and brought
to salt, to salt tears.

The scuttled ice floes move and shift
past the water's edge, beneath
the mountains of blue ice, ebbing
away. And we are moving. Sorrow
on the streets of Paris & Chicago

for the young ones slain and slain
and slain, we standing mute, staring
from our block of ice. The flowers
wilt, then blacken—
those memorials we keep adding to,

piled high as glaciers—

Making Snow Angels

This is no child's play, therefore:
to wave arms & legs back and forth
against a bank of thick snow

masking all sound, even my loud
laughter. I do my best to be heard,
even talking to myself—anything
to break this silence of Beguines.

I place mittened hands to my mouth—
the snow's taste fractured and bitter,
the others buried or drowned

wrecked   like fishes

"It snowed overnight . . ."

It snowed overnight & has covered
everything. The sharp cry of a bird
startles me awake.

The fire has gone out. I rise
to find the water in my basin
covered with a scrim of ice.
Impossible, that shimmer.
It soon cracks.

I am cold. I am paler than grass
as I kneel for morning prayer.
After that, a small breakfast
to be had. I cannot be seen
to eat. I cover my mouth
as I chew.

Winter: Mo(u)rning

Still as sorrow daylight
lies in waiting.

light rises. With day

comes fracture   space
for objects moving,

sudden car horns. Black night
to snowy dawns. Let snow

as Ceres does, mourning
her lost daughter   sowing
her seeds of corn

Snow

The snow comes down quickly.
It gathers on grass, on roof tiles.
It rushes toward its goal.

No time for vacillation,
veering back and forth
as snow sometimes does,
floating down
in the windless cold.

Do you love me or no?

So tenderly you held me—
I kissed your forehead
and tasted salt

"This is a major storm, it has life and death implications."

Nothing moves. Nothing can.
It is such an accident we're here.
It feels as if nothing *is* here.

The cold keeps to its own level.
The cold is the condition without which . . .

Houses set on fire. They burn.
They burn themselves out.

Farther Out

The trees have changed and even in
their leaflessness have softened
as has the blue sky overhead.

There are no clouds to speak of,
of trouble up ahead.

The past remains
a deeply scarred country.

Farther out is more unsteady quiet.
Farther out there are more sober plans.
Call it the pattern of the weather.

We must expect snow soon, and darkness.

Lot's Wife in Reverse

Looking at this land
she had never seen, the stars
and the new sky, her body
turned toward me, she freezes
to a statue in relief.

Lot's wife in reverse—she who
looked back and was cursed.

The others farther out
lick salt for luck
and make their exile's
journey to the shore.

ACKNOWLEDGMENTS

Several poems in this book have appeared previously (some in earlier versions) in the following print and online journals and collections:

The Avocet
Common Threads
Derelict Mansions (chapbook)
Earth Music
Pudding Magazine

My sincere thanks to Charles Portolano, poet and true friend of poets.

ABOUT THE AUTHOR

Eugene O'Connor, a native of Buffalo, New York, retired in 2017 from his position as Managing Editor and Acquiring Editor in Classics and Medieval Studies at The Ohio State University Press. His poems and translations have been published in *The Avocet, The Classical Bulletin, Classical Outlook, The Columbia Anthology of Gay Literature, Common Threads, The Comstock Review, Mead, Poetry Pacific, Pudding Magazine*, and elsewhere. His chapbook, *Derelict Mansions*, appeared in 2011.

Nature features in O'Connor's poems, often as a means of exploring human predation and folly. Even nature writ small—a twig, an insect perched on a leaf—can plumb larger, and darker, mysteries. In this O'Connor receives inspiration from past masters Emily Dickinson and Robert Frost.

Eugene O'Connor lives in Columbus, Ohio, with his partner, now husband, of thirty years.

www.ingramcontent.com/pod-product-compliance
Lightning Source LLC
Chambersburg PA
CBHW020703300426
44112CB00007B/504